The *New* Teacher's Guide to *Success*

A personalized planning guide
for beginning teachers

Author
Matthew Haldeman, M.Ed.

SHELL EDUCATION

The New Teacher's Guide to Success

Assistant Editor
Leslie Huber, M.A.

Senior Editor
Lori Kamola, M.S.Ed.

Editor-in-Chief
Sharon Coan, M.S.Ed.

Editorial Manager
Gisela Lee, M.A.

Creative Director
Lee Aucoin

Cover Design
Lee Aucoin

Interior Layout Designer
Robin Erickson

Print Production
Juan Chavolla

Publisher
Corinne Burton, M.A.Ed.

Shell Education
5301 Oceanus Drive
Huntington Beach, CA 92649-1030
www.shelleducation.com
ISBN 978-1-4258-0319-3
© 2008 Shell Education
Made in U.S.A.

Table of Contents

Introduction

I know what you're thinking: "Wait a minute! I'm not in school anymore. I'm done with worksheets, workbooks, tests, and quizzes. I'm the teacher now!"

Well, the truth is that being a teacher requires many times the preparation of being a student. You need to be well prepared to be successful.

I still remember my first day as a teacher. I had spent over $200 buying supplies I was sure I would need. I had taken classes on literacy instruction and classroom management. I had read through the districtwide standards and the teacher's edition of all my textbooks. I had even memorized the names of all my students. I was sure I was prepared.

I was completely wrong.

There were literally dozens of decisions that I had not even thought about. It had not crossed my mind where I would put the pencil sharpener, how far apart I wanted the desks to be, or what I would do if a student got angry and hit someone. I spent the rest of the school year making decisions that I should have thought about before the first day had even started.

The purpose of this planning guide is to make sure you are as prepared as possible when that first day comes. No matter how well prepared you think you are, there are probably some questions in this book you have not thought about. These are the types of issues that are learned through experience. I have pulled together a list of my experiences and the decisions I have been faced with as a teacher. I have also received input from many other excellent teachers. Together, this list of decisions and experiences formed the basis for this book. It is not expected that you should have all the answers right away; these decisions require thought and consideration.

This book is exactly what it claims to be: a planning guide. It is designed so you can write out the answers to the questions right here in the book. This may seem like a lot of work, but as any successful teacher will tell you, planning is most definitely worth the time it takes. Sooner or later, you will have to make a decision about each of the questions in this book. It is far better to start thinking about these issues now than to wait until the school year has already begun.

Ask a veteran teacher for advice on classroom management and you will get an earful. Experienced teachers often have good advice for rookies, but it may not always work. I call it the "You just gotta…" syndrome. Here are some of my favorites:

"You just gotta mean business."

"You just gotta show them who's boss."

"You just gotta wait them out."

"You just gotta set up routines."

"You just gotta call their parents."

What is problematic about this type of advice is that it makes teaching sound easier than it is. And, you will need to make decisions based on what you are comfortable with and what works for you. As a new teacher, I spent far too much time searching for that one answer that would solve everything. I treated teaching as if it were a mathematics problem that had one simple solution.

Of course, the more I taught, the more experience and confidence I gained. I soon realized how complex the job of being a teacher actually was. You need to have a variety of tools and tricks at your disposal for different situations. It takes time and patience to learn these strategies for success. It is not something you can learn to do in a weekend.

What used to bother me was that there were some teachers who never seemed to have any problems with their classes. If their methods worked for them, I wondered, why couldn't they work for me? I eventually learned that while it helps to use specific ideas you get from other teachers, it is usually not a good idea to copy them exactly. I learned to adapt these ideas to my specific classroom situation in order for them to work for my students.

What I've learned from watching other teachers and reading books on education is this: there is definitely more than one way to be successful at teaching. And thus, *The New Teacher's Guide to Success*, even though it is written for new teachers, will have almost no advice on how to teach. What I provide is a series of ideas to consider regarding the decisions you will have to make, along with the pros and cons of each choice. The rest is up to you. Taking time to thoroughly think about these situations will help you be more prepared for your first day of class and will help you increase your confidence. When your students see that you are confident, prepared, and organized, they will be more likely to respect your authority.

I am not saying that advice is overrated or that you cannot learn about teaching from reading a book or listening to someone. There are many excellent speakers and writers offering sound advice. What I *am* saying is that you cannot rely solely on what other people tell you. At some point, you will have to make your own decisions.

Just how complicated an endeavor is teaching? The quote by Donald D. Quinn on page 9 may give you some idea. There are so many decisions you must make each day. This book helps you consider your approach to some of these decisions ahead of time so that you'll be ready with a plan when the time comes.

You could, of course, just read the book and think about the questions it presents. This may seem like an enticing suggestion, especially as your summer winds down and you begin to feel pressed for time. I strongly urge you not to do this. It is highly unlikely that you will remember everything in this book without taking time to write down your ideas.

When you really think about it, you could probably finish this book in a day. That is one day over the summer that will save you many hours of decision making, when you won't have the time during the school year. During the school day, you will need to make choices quickly and confidently. Taking the time to think ahead now will help give you the confidence to trust in yourself and know that you are making good choices that work for you and your students.

When you are done with this book, don't put it away. Take it to school with you and use it as a reference book. Look through it often to remind yourself of your plans, and assess them as necessary.

It is likely that you will make changes along the way, but you will have a solid foundation to give you confidence and to be prepared to make decisions when you are faced with them.

Students trust and respond to teachers who are consistent. They respond well to routines and schedules if you establish them from the beginning. If you keep this book around, it will help ensure that you are following through with all the things you set out to do. If you need to make a change in plans along the way, then you should. You will see over time that flexibility is also very important as a teacher. With this book in hand, you will have a framework to help guide your decision-making process.

Remember: You are not doing any more work than you would have otherwise—you are just doing it before the school year starts.

"If a doctor, lawyer, or dentist had 40 people in his office at one time, all of whom had different needs, and some who didn't want to be there and were causing trouble, and the doctor or lawyer or dentist, without assistance, had to treat them all with professional excellence for nine months, then he might have some conception of the classroom teacher's job."
—Donald D. Quinn

Research

Across America, over 100,000 new teachers enter classrooms each fall. Many of these new teachers are not prepared to handle the challenges ahead. Of the new teachers that enter U.S. schools each year, most vary in their skills and experience. They also vary greatly in the amount of formal preparation they have had in anticipation of the serious responsibility of teaching. Why is it that so few of these teachers have received either the proper preparation or the thorough education necessary to be successful in the classroom? The following are some potential explanations for this incongruity: As a society, it often appears that we do not invest seriously in our children's education, especially those of a lower socioeconomic status. For many, the typical view of teaching is simplistic, conceived of as the teacher transmitting information to the student. Some may not understand the careful training required for successful teaching; others believe that there is not much to teaching beyond knowing the subject matter. Some licensing systems have entry requirements that lack serious standards, and educators have only recently agreed upon the necessary knowledge teachers should have before entering the classroom, as well as how that knowledge should be acquired (Darling-Hammond and Baratz-Snowden 2007).

As the above reasons would indicate, teacher preparation is an extremely relevant topic in the field of education today. *The Secretary's Fifth Annual Report on Teacher Quality* (U.S. Department of Education 2006) asserts that teacher quality is vital for student achievement, and quality seems directly proportional to adequate teacher preparation. During the 2003–04 school year, U.S. teacher preparation programs produced record numbers of teachers. More teachers are now required to complete preparation programs and pass standardized assessments.

What does research say about the benefits of teacher preparation? In "What Makes an Effective Teacher?," Ullik Rouk states that teacher preparation helps develop the knowledge and skill needed in the classroom. In addition, well-prepared teachers are more likely to continue teaching, as well as produce higher student achievement. The research shows that well-prepared teachers outperform those who are not; more specifically, they are able to diagnose a variety of learning needs, develop a positive classroom environment where students can thrive, and better apply strategies that promote success (1980).

This book, *The New Teacher's Guide to Success,* is designed to provide the tools necessary to prepare teachers for their first year in the classroom. It contains 10 chapters, each of which is designed to address a specific area of teaching that is pertinent for beginning teachers. These topics include teaching style, room environment, procedures and routines, behavior management, time management, parent communication, homework, assessment, organization, and the first days of class. *The New Teacher's Guide to Success* is suited for incoming teachers of all backgrounds and skill levels. Some teachers come prepared in their respective content areas but are unfamiliar with the other important aspects of teaching, such as curriculum, classroom management, and policies (Darling-Hammond and Baratz-Snowden 2007). This book asks prospective teachers to consider the facets of teaching outside their content areas so that they will be better acquainted with the business of *how* to teach, not simply *what* to teach.

In order to have a better sense of how to address the issues a first-time teacher will encounter, it helps to have a vision. A curricular vision involves teachers' ideas about where they are going and how they are going to get there—and more importantly, how to get students there. A solid vision often connects to important values and concrete practices that will help teachers develop their teaching styles and assess their students' learning (Darling-Hammond and Baratz-Snowden 2007). *The New Teacher's Guide to Success* is structured like a workbook so that beginning teachers can inquire about and reflect on their desired teaching experiences, thus creating unique visions of their own—those that will likely result in more positive classroom environments and increased student success.

How to Use This Book

Read through each chapter of the planning guide, starting at the beginning. This book is organized in a logical order to help you prepare for your first days of school. As you read each chapter, stop and think about how each strategy applies to you and your upcoming teaching situation. Each chapter asks you to reflect upon a specific aspect of your teaching and then take an active role in answering the questions for yourself. This method of inquiry will assist you in developing your teaching skills and strategies. Rather than simply taking in information, you have the opportunity to actively create your vision for teaching by answering the questions.

After you complete the book, go back and review each chapter, along with your answers to the questions. Decide whether you should change any answers now that you have had a chance to thoroughly think about the different strategies and situations.

After the school year starts, go back once again and review your answers. Use this book as a reference guide during the year to remind yourself of the goals you set and the decisions you made about your classroom. Add notes about what is working for you, what you've had to change or modify, and what you might do differently next year.

Teaching Style

1

There is certainly more than one way to be a good teacher. Different teachers have different teaching styles; there is no single right way to teach. The key is finding what teaching style, or combination of styles, works for you.

In the spaces below, you will have the opportunity to answer some questions about your teaching style. You will first read a description of a specific teaching style. Then you will think about how your teaching style is like the one described.

A Teacher Can Be:

The Disciplinarian—Being a disciplinarian does not mean you raise your voice or behave harshly toward students; it simply means that you have a set of consequences for every rule you have in place. The consequences could be a phone call home, a trip to the principal's office, or a low grade. The disciplinarian gets his or her students to listen because they know that if they don't adhere to the rules, there will be consequences.

To what extent am I like the disciplinarian?

_____

_____

The Caregiver—The caregiver became a teacher for one reason: to help students. If students are having problems, they know they can turn to this teacher, and they often do so even before going to their parents. This is the teacher who arrives early to tutor his or her students and stays after school to help struggling students or just to talk. This type of teacher boosts students' self-esteem and confidence so that students feel cared about. The caregiver's students often want to do well because they want to please their teacher, and they are able to focus on learning because their emotional needs have been met.

To what extent am I like the caregiver?

_____

_____

The Fun Lover—The fun lover knows how to make every lesson, including long division, boatloads of fun. This teacher writes plays, dresses up in wigs, sings songs, and does anything possible to get his or her students excited about the prospect of learning. These students may learn almost without realizing that they are learning. Even the troublemakers have so much fun that they don't think about creating a scene.

To what extent am I like the fun lover?

_____

_____

The Organizer—This teacher knows where everything is at the drop of a hat, and thus it is very difficult to pull anything over on him or her. If students walk in the door and say they don't have their homework, he or she will provide a worksheet and tell them to have it by tomorrow. If students are not paying attention in class, he or she will mark it down on a sheet and be sure to inform their parents that afternoon (or perhaps even during lunch). Pretty soon, most kids stop trying to fool the teacher; they know it will only lead to more work.

To what extent am I like the organizer?

_____

_____

The Community Creator—The students in this teacher's class know that the room is its own community with its own rules and privileges. It is a place where they feel safe and where they can act without fear of being judged. This teacher has made it clear that everyone in the classroom is working together to be successful.

To what extent am I like the community creator?

_____

_____

> *"Many things are important for good schools: curriculum...parent involvement... a clean, safe building...but of all the things that are important...nothing is as important as the teacher and what that person knows, believes, and can do."*
> *—Jon Saphier and Robert Gower*

Room Environment

Setting up your room is the first thing you will have to think about as a teacher. Think about how you will teach. Do you plan to have students work in cooperative groups? Do you need space for students to sit on the floor for read-aloud time? Will you have centers? Can you move around the room? You can change your floor plan during the year, but the tone you set with your room environment at the beginning of the year is important. The room environment will change depending on what grade level you teach; for example, a kindergarten classroom will likely be set up with more activity centers, as well as more open floor space for group work and instruction.

Room Setup

Accessibility: Your classroom is a place to store books, pencils, paper, art supplies, coats, book bags, lunches, student portfolios, your personal items, and much, much more. How easy is it for you (or one of your students) to get to any of these items? You want to make this as easy as possible.

Visibility: When the school year starts, your walls will be filled with important information that you will want your students to know. Is every student in a place where he or she can see the bulletin boards, the blackboard, and you, the teacher? The easiest way to lose a student's attention is to seat him or her someplace where he or she cannot really see.

Mobility: A good teacher is constantly moving around the room to interact with students. Likewise, your students are going to have to get out of their seats for a variety of reasons: to use the restroom, to sharpen their pencils, to exit the room for a fire drill, etc. Is it easy to move around in your classroom?

Flexibility: You will probably be doing a variety of activities in your classroom, including lectures, tests, group work, and projects. Different activities require different seating arrangements. How easy will it be for you to rearrange the classroom if you need to?

Things to Consider

Will you have a classroom library? If so, where in the room will it be? How will you organize it?

_____

_____

_____

Will you have computers? Where will they be? Can they be moved elsewhere if necessary?

_____

_____

_____

Does your school have any requirements about things you must have in your room? If so, what are these things and where might you place them?

Some schools have very specific requirements about room setup, including the location of centers, the number and size of bulletin boards, seating arrangements, etc.

_____

_____

_____

Where is the most natural place for you to stand while you are teaching? Do you feel comfortable moving around the room?

You will, of course, be moving around a lot of the time. It still makes sense, however, to have a home base to come back to from time to time. Choose a place that is close to either a blackboard or an overhead projector and also somewhere that all your students will be able to see without craning their necks.

_____

_____

Is there a place where students can put their book bags and coats? Is it away from a main traffic area? Is the location one that will create a visual distraction for students seated nearby? Describe this area.

Do not underestimate the mess that bags, coats, lunches, jump ropes, and basketballs can create in a classroom. If there is no closet for these things, you may want students to take the items to their own desks, as long as they don't get in the way.

_____

_____

_____

Will you have a desk? Where is it located? Are you able to move it if you want to?

Carefully consider where you would place a desk so as not to interfere with the interaction between you and your students. Don't place it where it may impede your ability to walk around the room or observe class behavior; it is important to remain in close proximity to your students at all times.

_____

_____

Do you have a place (a closet or a file cabinet) to store the following things: personal belongings, student files/work to show parents, student work that hasn't been graded yet, additional supplies? Is there some way you can lock this space?

_____

_____

Where will you place your bulletin boards?

Does your school want you to have individual bulletin boards for each subject? Keep in mind that some spaces are more prominent than others. You will have to make a decision about which bulletin boards are the most important.

_____

_____

_____

Where do you plan to post your rules, consequences, and procedures (e.g., fire alarm procedure)? Why is it important for you to post written material in these locations?

_____

_____

_____

If other teachers come in during the day, will they have a space that is their own? If so, where will this be? If not, how do you plan to share your work space with them?

Having a space for mobile teachers (e.g., reading specialists) will show that you value the work they are doing in your room. It shows that you view them as collaborative partners.

_____

_____

_____

Does your classroom meet all fire and safety codes?

_____

_____

Do you plan to set up centers in your classroom? If so, how do you intend to organize these? Where will each be located?

Centers are places that students can work independently. Some teachers work rotating centers into their daily lessons, some reserve them for students who finish early, and some do not use them at all. If you are going to use them, remember that they do require a lot of space. A writing center would need paper, pencils, a place to post a writing prompt, and space for at least two students. If you are setting up activity centers for younger students (K–2), you will need to plan for the additional materials needed at such stations.

_____

_____

_____

Is there a space for students who need quiet places to work or read?

This is not intended for the student who is being disruptive. Some students simply prefer some time to themselves, especially when doing a quiet activity like reading or writing. Students often like to know that there is a place in the classroom they can go if the person sitting next to them is being disruptive. This allows them to avoid confrontation on their own.

_____

_____

Seating Arrangements

In the traditional classroom setting, students sat in rows. Nobody really questioned it or suggested other options. Today, walking through most schools, every type of seating arrangement imaginable can be seen. You will want to find out if your school or district has guidelines on seating arrangements. On the following pages are some diagrams with the possible advantages and limitations of each arrangement.

The other important decision you have to make is what type of teaching is going to go on in your room. You cannot very well set up your room until you know what is going to be taking place inside it. Before you look at the diagrams, review the chart on the following page to see how seating arrangements are connected to teaching styles and goals for the class.

Consider these questions: Will your students be working in groups? How big will those groups be? Will you have space in the back for centers? Will you have space for anything else (e.g., a place to hold meetings, a cozy place to read)? What will you do if additional students are added to your class? Students often learn better in groups, but groups can also lead to off-task talking. You need to decide how big you want the groups to be. Ideally, you should keep your groups relatively small; however, it can be hard to keep track of too many small groups. If necessary, try it out a few different ways to see what works best for your class.

Three Types of Teaching

	Features	Arrangement	Benefits
1. Lecture	The entire class observes the teacher.	All chairs face the front of the classroom.	Note-taking is a priority. Talking is at a minimum.
2. Discussion	The entire class participates in the same activity.	Chairs are usually in a circle or an oval.	Everyone is able to see and hear one another.
3. Group	Students work in groups of 2, 3, 4, or 5.	Chairs and tables are placed in groups.	Groups are spaced apart so as not to disturb each other.

"The purpose of arranging seats is to accomplish classroom tasks."
—Harry and Rosemary Wong

Three Types of Seating Arrangements

Lecture

This setup allows for a small amount of group work, but is best for a lecture-driven type of class. This setup also helps minimize talking because students are facing the front of the classroom. The walkway down the center makes it easy for the teacher to get to every student.

 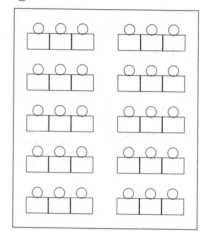

Discussion

This setup is neither group focused nor lecture focused. The advantage of this structure is that it is flexible. The teacher can work with the center group or call students up from their individual work as he or she sees fit.

 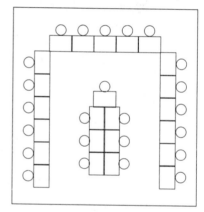

Group

This setup is group focused. The number of desks per group is varied because some students work better in smaller groups. Even though the focus is on group work, none of the students has his or her back to the teacher. Note how all the desks are centered on a single point from which the teacher can speak.

 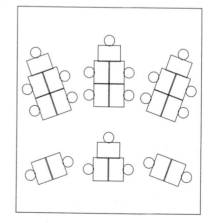

What My Classroom Will Look Like

Use this space to draw what you would like your classroom to look like.

Now that your room is set up, take a moment to walk around. Ask yourself the following questions:

Can I move around the classroom with ease?	
Will all students be able to see me while I teach?	
Can every student see the bulletin boards from where he or she is sitting?	
Can every student get in and out of his or her seat easily?	
Will it be difficult to move from one activity to another?	
Is this a room my students will be comfortable in for the next nine months?	
Is this a room I will be comfortable in?	

If you can answer yes to each of these questions, then your room is ready for your students!

Procedures and Routines

3

   This is a critical section of the book. It is also an area of teaching that needs to be carefully addressed by first-year teachers.

   It is easy to see why. Do your students really need to be taught how to enter a classroom, how to sharpen a pencil, or how to raise their hands to use the bathroom? Yes, they do. Even if they are 10 or 11 years old? Absolutely!

   Every question on the pages that follow represents a procedure or routine that you will need to teach to your new class. You will want to make sure they know the routines and procedures for your classroom. You need to model these routines and have students practice them until they become just that—routine. Students respond well to routines, and this helps to control order in your classroom. When you have a smoothly running class, then you can focus on teaching, and your students can focus on learning.

   You are a new teacher—you cannot change that. But you can control your level of preparation. If you are prepared and if you let students know of your expectations, then you are setting yourself up for success.

Schedule

Will you have a daily schedule posted? If so, what will it look like? Will this schedule be provided to and discussed with parents? If so, how?

A daily class schedule may help students be more prepared for class. Since students generally thrive on structure, this can be a great tool for success. You might also consider sending a letter home to parents that shares your class schedule with them so that they can better assist their children in preparing for class.

_____

_____

_____

Officers and Monitors

Will you have officers or monitors to help reinforce the rules and procedures? If so, how will you use them? How will you hold them accountable for their positions? How will you develop respect for these roles among your students? Where will you post jobs and officer names?

Assign jobs to students to assist with the rules and procedures for the class. This helps keep things running smoothly and gives students a sense of responsibility. Jobs may be changed weekly or monthly to allow all students to have a turn. Job descriptions should be discussed and reinforced at the start of the year. Examples may include a line leader, library monitor, center monitor, and attendance monitor.

_____

_____

_____

Arrival

How do you want your students to enter the room? Is the room arranged to allow for flow on entering and exiting? What problems do you anticipate?

_____

_____

_____

Do you want students to line up outside your door? Is it okay for them to talk as they come in? If a student enters the room inappropriately, will you have him or her re-enter? How late is acceptable, and how late is too late? Should they sit down immediately in their chairs, or do you want them to stand behind their seats and wait for you to seat them? How do you plan to make this clear to them?

Students often enjoy role-playing. You can pick two students and have one of them demonstrate the wrong way to enter the class and have one of them show the correct way. Repetition is key; have your students practice walking in and out of class.

Morning Routine

What is your morning routine?

This is also something you will want to emphasize to your students during the first week of school. Consider posting it in the classroom where it can be easily referred to throughout the year. Refer to the next page for an example of a morning routine.

1. _____

2. _____

3. _____

4. _____

5. _____

Example of a Morning Routine:

1. Hang up your coat.

2. Put your book bag in your locker.

3. Turn in your homework.

4. Sharpen your pencil.

5. Begin the morning activity.

What will be the first activity of the day?

Make sure students have something they must complete in the mornings before class starts. It is a good idea to post these morning assignments in the same place every day. Possible suggestions: check your homework, write in your journal, silent reading time, practice math flashcards, etc. The important thing is to make sure you don't have any students arriving in the morning with nothing to do. When students have an activity to start on right away, they are more likely to be focused and ready for the day.

_____

_____

_____

Will your students have assigned seats? How will you keep track of this?

Assigned seats are usually a good idea. You may want to group students by ability, have students of mixed abilities working together, or just make sure no student is sitting next to someone he or she is likely to talk to. Keep a seating chart close by for situations when someone else is in your classroom, such as a substitute teacher.

_____

_____

_____

Will you use nameplates in your class? What will they look like, and where will you put them?

You may want to use nameplates at the start of the new school year to help you and the students get to know each other. Consider whether you want to place them on the top of student desks or tape them in front. There are a number of different designs you could use for these (e.g., My name is _____.; Reserved for special student _____.). Be creative!

_____

_____

_____

How will you take roll and still keep track of what is going on in your classroom?

This is an important question to consider, especially in the beginning. Some teachers like to hand this job over to a responsible student, while others take roll while students are working on their morning activity. There are several different ways to take roll, but whichever you choose, be sure roll is taken quickly so you can get on with your day.

_____

_____

Dismissal

What steps will your dismissal procedure include?

As with the morning routine, you may want to post this procedure somewhere in the classroom so that students can refer to it easily. See below for an example of a dismissal procedure.

1. _____

2. _____

3. _____

4. _____

5. _____

Example of a Dismissal Procedure:

1. Copy down your assignments.
2. Collect your coat and bag.
3. Put back library books.
4. Stack your chair.
5. Line up.

What signal will you give students to begin the dismissal procedure? How will you monitor the dismissal procedure?

_____

_____

_____

Will students leave in groups upon dismissal?

With large classes, it can sometimes get crowded if everyone goes to the closet, coatrack, or cubby area at the same time. You may want to have a way of dismissing them in smaller groups to avoid this problem. Consider dismissing students based on which groups/rows are the quietest, which know the answer to a question, and so on.

How will you ensure that the room is clean?

Some teachers hold all of the students accountable for cleaning up the room. Some wait for students to clean their own personal areas and dismiss them separately. Some designate helpers whose job it is to make sure the room is clean. You might consider having students line up for dismissal in the order in which they finish cleaning up their area. Note: Using mild hand wipes are a great way to keep the room clean, including desks, supplies, and students' hands.

Transitions

For self-contained classroom teachers (e.g., elementary school, special education): How will you move from one activity to the next?

Careful management of transition time between lessons can maximize teaching time. Have a set procedure for transitions. Not only will this shorten the time between subjects but it will also ensure that all students know what their roles are. Consider using attention signals or quiet signals for these transitions (e.g., raising a hand, turning off the lights, clapping out a rhythm).

For single-subject teachers: How will you ensure that the class that is leaving does not interfere with the incoming class?

If you have two doors in your room, you may want to label one of them an entering door and one of them an exiting door. If you don't have two doors, you may want to have the incoming class line up outside your classroom.

_____

_____

Movement

Under what circumstances may students get out of their seats? How will you provide for typical movement needs of students during the day?

There will likely be occasions when students get out of their seats when they should be focusing on a specific learning activity. This can be reduced by keeping your students actively engaged in learning. You will want to make sure you have a system in place for when students get out of their seats. Refer to Chapter 4 for ideas on developing a behavior management system.

_____

_____

_____

Do you have a pass or a sign-out sheet for when students need to leave the classroom? Under what conditions will these be given to students?

_____

_____

_____

What should I do if…

…a student has to go to the bathroom?

To maximize instruction time, try using hand signals for students who have to use the restroom. Teach them to raise their fists or cross their fingers. You can give them a nod, and they can go without disrupting the class.

_____

_____

…a student is feeling sick?

_____

_____

…a student needs to sharpen a pencil?

_____

_____

…a student needs to throw something away?

_____

_____

…a student is visibly angry or upset?

You can help students develop the skills to recognize when they are angry and need some space. You may want to encourage (or even require) them to go to a designated place in the classroom to cool down when they feel angry or upset.

_____

_____

Noise Level

How will you get your students' attention?

You will want to use a signal like "1, 2, 3, all eyes on me!" or a hand in the air, or a quick countdown from 10 to indicate to your students that you want them to stop talking and look at you. If you always use the same signal, it will quickly become a habit. See other examples of attention signals in the Transitions section (page 33).

_____

_____

_____

When are students allowed to talk?

_____

_____

_____

When are they allowed to talk quietly or whisper?

_____

_____

_____

When are they not allowed to talk at all?

_____

_____

_____

How will you clarify and explain distinctions among these scenarios in a way your students can understand?

Students can get confused as to why talking is sometimes encouraged and sometimes discouraged. Some teachers like to post a picture of a stoplight in their classroom. If they point to red, they expect silence (e.g., during silent reading time). If they point to yellow, students are allowed to whisper quietly with a partner. If they point to green, it is time for group work and students can talk about their specific learning activities.

_____

_____

What should students do if they have a question or want to offer a response to a question?

Students should be encouraged to ask questions. The trick is letting them know the appropriate time to ask them. When you ask questions, sometimes you will want your students to call out the answer, and sometimes you will want them to raise their hands. It can be difficult for students, especially young ones, to understand the difference. Spend some time explaining your expectations.

_____

_____

_____

What are your rules on talking during an assembly?

_____

_____

What about talking before and after class?

_____

_____

Walking in the Hallways

Will you have one line or two? _____

Some teachers like to divide their students into separate lines so that each line is shorter, allowing them to more easily see all the students at once.

Are students allowed to talk in line?_____

It is common policy in many schools to have a no-talking policy while walking in the halls to avoid disrupting other classrooms.

Will you walk in front of, in back of, or in the middle of the line?_____

Try out each one. There are advantages and limitations to each.

Will you have a line leader?_____

Will you have a door holder?_____

Will you have someone in the back of the line to make sure all students are accounted for?_____

How will you designate these positions?

See the Officers and Monitors section (page 28) for ideas on designating jobs/positions to students.

_____

_____

_____

In what order will the students line up? Will you always have them line up in the same way?

Some teachers have their students line up by height. Others have them line up by group. Some allow students who are quietest to line up first. Some have a rotating list of positions, such as line leader. Choose a system that works for you and your students.

_____

_____

_____

"The number one problem in the classroom is not discipline; it is the lack of procedures and routines."

—Harry and Rosemary Wong

Behavior Management

Ask any teacher what the most important part of teaching is and the answer will almost always be classroom management or behavior management. There is a crucial difference between managing a classroom and disciplining a classroom. Managing a classroom means creating a consistent structure for students; this allows them to be productive and feel safe in their learning environment. Discipline alone implies punishment and control. Developing a management system that includes rules, consequences, and rewards means that positive reinforcement encourages good behavior, and negative behavior is a result of students' choices and is therefore treated with the appropriate (and agreed-upon) consequences.

Rules

The first rule of rule-setting is this: Rules are not mean. They are necessary.

Rules are necessary because they set boundaries. Your students need to know what behavior is acceptable in your class and what is not. More importantly, rules help other students in the class feel safe and protected.

Classroom rules should be:

- short
- few in number
- in language students understand
- positive
- posted in your classroom
- distributed to students
- communicated to parents

Problematic Rules

- Try your best! (this is a motto)
- Raise your hand to use the bathroom! (this is a procedure)
- Don't run! (negative)
- Listen! (too vague)

You can help your students view their actions as choices. If students violate a rule, they have made a choice—they have *chosen* to break a rule.

Some teachers like to have their students help them make up the rules. They believe that this helps students take ownership of the rules. If you choose to involve your students in developing a set of classroom rules, it is usually a good idea to know ahead of time what rules you are looking for. Then, you can help guide your students' thinking toward those rules while you are brainstorming.

Either way, your students must agree that the rules are fair. If they view the rules as fair, they will be more likely to follow them.

My Classroom Rules

1. _____

2. _____

3. _____

4. _____

5. _____

Possible Rules

- Always listen and talk respectfully to others.
- Keep your hands to yourself.
- Follow directions the first time they are given.
- Treat others as you would like to be treated.

Things to Consider

Where will you post your rules? _____

Will you write them or will your students write them?

_____

How will you ensure that your students will follow the rules?

_____

_____

_____

Can you think of any negative behaviors not covered by your rules? What will you do if a student displays this type of behavior?

_____

_____

_____

Does your school have its own set of rules? How can you ensure that your rules are not in conflict with the school rules?

_____

_____

_____

Do your rules apply to behavior on the playground, in the cafeteria, and in the hallway, or are they only for the classroom?

_____

_____

_____

Will other teachers who teach your class have a different set of rules? How will you help your students distinguish between the two?

This is something you might want to discuss with the other teachers ahead of time. Often, teachers who have the same class get together and adopt a universal set of rules.

_____

_____

_____

Are your rules:

- short? _____
- few in number? _____
- easy for students to understand? _____
- positive? _____
- posted in your classroom? _____

> **"The standards in any classroom are defined by whatever the student can get away with."**
>
> **—Fred Jones**

Consequences

When a student breaks a rule, there must be a consequence for that action. If there is a posted consequence and the teacher is consistent in following through, then the student who breaks a rule has no reason to be angry with the teacher. He or she has chosen to break a rule and must accept the consequences.

Students will only accept your system of consequences if they are consistent and logical. If you do not apply your consequences to every student in every situation, you will be accused of favoritism. If your consequences are not logical, students will also not accept them.

Most consequences are for the individual student, but some involve the entire class. For instance, some teachers tell their students that if they cannot walk down the hallway without talking, they will go back and do it again. In this case, if one student misbehaves, the whole class accepts the consequence. This method allows you to use the influence of students' peers to obtain a positive result.

As you write your consequences, make sure they are things you are willing to carry out every day, or even several times a day if necessary. You may also want to enlist your students' help in coming up with consequences.

First-year teachers may be tempted to ease up on consequences because they want to be liked by their students. In reality, failure to deliver on your consequences will more often make you look lenient and incompetent. It is important to establish and maintain a relationship of mutual respect between you and your students; this is largely accomplished by following through with consequences.

My Consequences

1. _____   6. _____

2. _____   7. _____

3. _____   8. _____

4. _____   9. _____

5. _____   10. _____

Possible Consequences

time-out	be the last to leave	warning
write a note of apology	loss of recess	clean the room
after-school detention	suspension	redo the task
in-class detention	expulsion	note home
a phone call home	loss of reward	
principal's office	redo the assignment	

Things to Consider

How can you convince your students that your system of consequences is logical?

Whether they come up with the consequences themselves or you simply explain it to them, your students need to believe in your system.

_____

_____

_____

How can you administer your consequences without breaking the flow of your lesson?

It is important that you can deal with minor problems while still teaching. Some teachers place checks by students' names or move cards with their names on them. Just be sure you have already established what the consequences are. These methods have the same end result: the student is disciplined with minimal disruption to the class.

_____

_____

_____

How can you ensure that you have the support of the administration?

_____

_____

_____

How can you ensure you have parental support?

Consider sending home a letter outlining your classroom rules and consequences to enlist support from parents. Be sure to include a space for both the parent and the student to sign, signifying that they have read and understand all the rules. You might also have students create their own list of the class rules. This way, they can keep it with them as a reminder of the behavior that will help them succeed. You can also make phone calls to parents in place of a letter.

_____

_____

_____

What will you do if your system of consequences is not working for the class?

_____

_____

_____

What will you do if your system of consequences is not working for one student?

Some students may not care about any of your consequences or may decide that the thrill they get from breaking your rules is worth the consequences. Some teachers create individualized action plans for those students who are immune to the classroom consequences. These plans are a personalized system of rewards and consequences for the individual. Individual action plans can include any number of the following: independent work in lieu of group work, a letter home, a student progress form, work/ behavior contract, or notice of missing/overdue work. Be sure to include a space for parent signatures when appropriate.

_____

_____

_____

Rewards

Almost all teachers have some system of consequences in their classrooms. Also consider a reward system. Students respond favorably to rewards for good behavior. When you recognize good behavior and point it out, you encourage more good behavior.

Some teachers believe that the only rewards a student should strive for are good grades and a pat on the back. They insist that by offering incentives such as stickers, food, free time, trips, and parties, we are simply bribing our students to do well.

However, other teachers use systems of rewards very effectively. They believe that if they are going to have a system of consequences when students behave poorly, they also need to have a system of rewards when students behave well. Furthermore, these teachers often find creative ways to offer rewards without spending very much time or money.

My Rewards

Individual

1. _____

2. _____

3. _____

4. _____

Classroom

1. _____

2. _____

3. _____

4. _____

Examples of Rewards

Rewards That Take Up Your Time

- making phone calls

- writing notes

- organizing a trip or party

- playing games or watching a video after school

- extra recess

- certificates

Good for One No Homework

Rewards That Cost Money

- snacks
- pencils
- stickers
- erasers
- toys
- fancy pens
- trips
- sharpeners
- parties
- trinkets
- food
- folders
- books
- games

Simple Rewards

- a smile
- extra credit/bonus points
- student of the month
- praise
- words of encouragement
- a special job
- special privileges (e.g., no-homework token, extra free time, library pass, computer time, special helper of the day, special project)

Student of the Month

One of the simplest and most effective ways to reward students is with positive reinforcement, or verbal praise. The following are examples of different ways to use verbal praise with your students:

- I like the way you handled that.
- I'm glad you enjoy learning.
- I'm glad you are pleased with this.
- It looks as if you enjoyed doing this.
- Wow! Your effort really shows here.
- I have confidence in you.
- Thanks, you helped a lot.
- It was thoughtful of you to…
- Thanks, you just made my job a lot easier.
- You have a knack for…
- You do a good job of…
- I really enjoyed working with you. Thanks!
- You have really improved in…
- Keep up the good work.

You can also give praise in the form of certificates, awards, and tickets. These may include paper bookmarks, certificates of appreciation or completed work, and complimentary tickets that can later be exchanged for small prizes.

Things to Consider

Do you plan to have a system of rewards? Why or why not?

_____

_____

_____

How will you make sure you don't break the bank?

An easy way to avoid spending a lot of money is to give out tickets for a drawing so you only have to buy one prize. Think creatively about awards you can give out that cost little to no money.

_____

_____

_____

How will you make sure you don't spend too much time on rewards?

Again, be creative. Often, younger students enjoy doing tasks such as sorting papers, cleaning your room, or taking notes down to the office. If this is the case, your rewards system can actually help save you time.

_____

_____

_____

Will you use individual rewards, group rewards, or both?

One added advantage of group awards is positive peer influence. Students will work hard to keep their classmates on track.

_____

_____

_____

How will you inform parents that their child has received an award?

Try to let parents know when their child has done something positive. If they hear about the positive things, they will be more receptive to listening when you call about poor behavior. You might consider sending certificates home to inform parents of goals reached and/or good behavior.

_____

_____

_____

Will rewards be given out for specific actions, or just randomly?

Some teachers simply give out rewards at random. Other teachers outline very specifically what students need to do in order to earn a reward. Refer to the Rewards section (pages 49–51) for examples.

_____

_____

_____

Time Management

One challenge of teaching is that there is no set amount of time you have to work. When the school day ends, there is so much else that needs to be done: planning standards-based lessons, grading papers, planning field trips, and so on. The key is to prioritize your tasks to make your time well spent.

After all, if you had unlimited time to devote to teaching, think of what you could do! If you had unlimited time to plan your lessons, you could make each lesson so entertaining that every student would be on the edge of his or her seat.

But obviously, you do not have that luxury. When the school day ends, you need time to unwind, maybe exercise, and definitely sleep. These things are not optional. Many first-year teachers with good intentions want to master it all in their first year. They are so determined to excel that they sacrifice personal time and even sleep.

On one hand, this is impressive; these teachers are clearly sacrificing for their students. But these hardworking teachers can burn out quickly. They survive without sleep or free time for a few weeks or even a month, but soon they are so worn out that they collapse after a hard day at school. They spend all weekend in bed recovering. Before long, they are actually getting less work done than they would have if they had paced themselves from the beginning.

Think of teaching as a journey. You will be learning and refining your skills as you go.

Be flexible and forgiving with your schedule. You might tell yourself that you need two hours to plan each lesson, or that you must do five hours of grading each night. Sometimes you have to accept the fact that you cannot always do it all—at least not every day. You can start by making a schedule for yourself with what you want to accomplish each day or week. Pay attention to the activities that consume your time—if they are not productive, then you may want to re-evaluate your schedule.

The following questions ask you to think about how you spend your time each day. In addition to working, eating, sleeping, and making time for yourself, you will have to set aside time for grading, lesson planning, etc. All of these things are important—in fact, personal time is one of the most important parts of the day because it keeps you feeling refreshed and ready for the next busy day! Carefully consider how much time you spend on each activity, and remember—you can't always fit it all in, but planning will make it easier to manage your time and meet your goals.

Time Management Questions

A. How long is your school day? Include travel time, but don't include free periods during the day. _____

B. What is the minimum amount of sleep you need per night? _____

C. How much time do you need each day for running errands, paying bills, grocery shopping, doing laundry, attending class, spending time with your family/friends/children, etc.? _____

D. How much time do you need for preparing and eating meals, as well as cleaning up after your meals? _____

E. What is the minimum personal time you need each day to ensure that you are refreshed for the next day? (Do not answer zero.) _____

F. What activities fall into the category of personal time?
   Suggested answers: exercise, television, video games,
   talking on the phone, hanging out with friends, shopping,
   going for walks. (Write down as many as apply.)

_____   _____

_____   _____

_____   _____

On the letters below, write the number of hours you listed for
each activity on p. 56 (A–E). Calculate the total. Now subtract
the total from 24, and you can see how much time you have left in
your day to devote to planning and improving your teaching skills.
Decide what is most important for you to focus on. It is advisable
to focus on one or two areas/things. Try to choose reasonable
goals. When you accomplish them, celebrate and then choose
new goals.

$$\overline{A} + \overline{B} + \overline{C} + \overline{D} + \overline{E} = \underline{\qquad}$$

$$24 - \underline{\qquad\qquad\qquad\qquad} = \underline{\qquad\qquad\qquad\qquad}$$
$$\quad\qquad (A + B + C + D + E) \qquad\qquad \text{hours left for teaching prep.}$$

Planning and Prioritizing

There are several ways you can prepare for the next day. Take a look at the list below. There are many different tasks that teachers are responsible for.

Important Tasks

- plan for the next day
- grade homework
- grade tests
- make phone calls to parents
- put grades in grade book
- follow through with consequences
- perform administrative duties
- decorate room
- set up bulletin board
- clean room
- apply for grants
- plan field trips
- attend conferences
- read educational books

Planning and preparing for the next day is a question of priority. Some teachers spend three hours after school working on posters and bulletin boards for their rooms. Then they go home and are too exhausted to write effective lesson plans. A well-planned lesson is more important than a nice-looking bulletin board.

When faced with a list of tasks, most people tend to do the ones they like first and leave the less enjoyable tasks for last. Rank your tasks in order of priority and do the most important tasks first. That way, if you run out of time, at least you will have completed the important tasks.

Which of these tasks is the most important? That is up to you to decide. Many teachers would probably say that planning for the next day is the most important. They would say that it is the one thing on the list that cannot be put off until the next day.

Other teachers would say that the first thing they do is follow through with consequences. They would say that if you promise a student that you'll call his or her house or give him or her a detention, that should be your priority. Prioritizing is about being realistic.

Things to Consider

Which of the main tasks will be most important for you? Why?

_____

_____

_____

Which of the peripheral tasks will be most important? Why?

_____

_____

_____

Are you a perfectionist? If so, how do you see this affecting your time management?

_____

_____

_____

How will you ensure that you don't spend too much time on any one task?

_____

_____

_____

Can your students help you complete any of these tasks?

As stated in the Rewards section (page 52), students often enjoy doing things such as setting up bulletin boards, filing papers, cleaning your room, decorating your room, or even grading. If you are really creative, you can even find a way to incorporate these tasks into the learning process.

_____

_____

_____

Do you engage in any activities that are not productive and do not refresh you for the next day? How can you refocus or eliminate these activities?

_____

_____

_____

When choosing in what order to do certain tasks, do not let your enjoyment of the task (or lack thereof) enter into the decision-making process!

Weekly Schedule

The planner on the following page will allow you to organize your nights and weekends. Try to be as detailed as possible. List the most important things first and recognize that you may not be able to get to everything. In addition to a weekly schedule, consider creating a daily task book, along with the status of each task (e.g., completed, in progress). It might also be helpful to create task books for the beginning of the year, the end of the year, and meetings.

Things to Consider

Will you have a daily task book? If so, how will you organize it?

_____

_____

_____

Will you have any additional task books to help you organize the school year? What will these look like?

_____

_____

_____

Weekly Planner

Things to complete on Monday night

1. _____
2. _____
3. _____
4. _____
5. _____

Things to complete on Tuesday night

1. _____
2. _____
3. _____
4. _____
5. _____

Things to complete on Wednesday night

1. _____
2. _____
3. _____
4. _____
5. _____

Things to complete on Thursday night

1. _____
2. _____
3. _____
4. _____
5. _____

Weekend Activities

1. _____
2. _____
3. _____
4. _____
5. _____
6. _____
7. _____
8. _____
9. _____
10. _____

Parent Communication

Good parent communication is an important part of being an effective teacher. Keeping the lines of communication open will help you establish a relationship as partners in teaching. The following are two key ideas to communicate to parents:

- Their child's teacher and school want them to be involved.

- They will be regularly informed and updated on their child's progress, both in areas that they excel and in areas that they need assistance.

It is up to you to decide exactly how you are going to convey the above messages to parents. Some teachers prefer to make home visits. They feel that this gives them the best opportunity to get to know their students' families and vice versa. However, home visits require a significant time commitment and can thus be challenging for middle- and high-school teachers with 150 students.

Phone calls are another effective way of keeping in touch with parents, but can also be time consuming. Writing letters, sending emails, and allowing students to take their work home are three strategies that take less time and can still have a positive impact.

All parents:

- think their children are special
- like getting positive reports
- worry about their children from the minute they walk out the door

Some parents:

- have unrealistic ideas of their children's abilities
- can get defensive very easily

Also decide what you are going to do if a parent has concerns. It is not uncommon for parents to think that their children are being treated unfairly, were given an unfair grade, or were punished for something they did not do.

When talking to parents or writing comments/notes home about their child, be careful about how you express yourself. Avoid value judgments. Instead, focus on specific behavior. For example:

Don't say: "Juan is lazy."	**Do say:** "Juan didn't do his work today."
Don't say: "Analisa is violent."	**Do say:** "Analisa pushed a girl in gym."
Don't say: "Liam is a liar."	**Do say:** "Liam told me he did his work, but he never handed it in."

Another important aspect of contacting parents is discussing ways that they can help out at home. The following are examples of how parents can support their child's education at home:

- Review books and papers at home with your child. Show interest in his or her work; this communicates the idea that education is important.

- Talk with your child daily about school, everyday happenings, and current events.

- Instruct your child to finish homework earlier in the day rather than leaving it until the last minute.

- Provide a quiet, well-lit area where your child can study. Set up an area designated for study, and provide materials for your child to work with.

- Insist that homework be done away from the television and other potential distractions. Some individuals work better with background music, while others find it distracting. Find out what works best for your child.

- Take an interest in your child's schoolwork and provide additional help when he or she has an upcoming test. It is also helpful to quiz your child orally on the information he or she is currently studying.

- If your child has trouble understanding something, try to help.

- Be aware of study strategies such as note-taking that can be shared with your child.

- Read with your child and around your child. Encourage your child to read for pleasure. Discuss what your child reads independently and what you read together.

Things to Consider

How and when will you gather contact information for parents (address, phone number, email address, etc.)?

_____

_____

_____

How often will you call parents? When will you call? Where do parents prefer to be called—at home or at work?

Calling parents when a child misbehaves is an excellent behavior-management technique. However, parents are often resentful when the only contact they have with their child's teacher is when he or she does something wrong. If you have already made a habit of calling, it will be easier to pick up the phone when there is a challenging situation.

_____

_____

_____

Will you send out a welcome letter or packet? What will this include? Will you send out other letters periodically? How often? What form will these letters take?

An introductory letter to parents can be helpful in establishing a relationship with them at the beginning of the year. You might include your expectations of the parent(s) and the student, additional information you would like to have about the student (e.g., special needs, allergies, study habits), and contact information. Other letters or forms that you might send home during the year include student progress forms, volunteer forms (to give parents the opportunity to volunteer at school), a thank-you letter for those parents who offer their time, and a weekly or monthly newsletter outlining recent class activities, assignments, etc.

_____

_____

_____

What information is most important for parents to know?

Parents like to be kept informed about as many things as possible. Sending out letters is far easier than calling each one individually. In addition, letters will protect you against the parent who comes up with the excuse, "You never told me."

_____

_____

_____

What will you do if a parent feels a situation is unfair?

_____

_____

_____

What will you do if a child does something that you do not allow and tells you, "My mother/father said I could"?

_____

_____

_____

How will you handle a child whose parents are uninvolved or unavailable, despite your best efforts?

_____

_____

_____

How will you handle special cases (e.g., communicating with parents who have joint custody)?

_____

_____

_____

Homework

Keeping up with your grading can be a huge challenge. If you have 25 students and each student does a page of math, a page of reading, and a page of social studies for homework (this will vary depending on what grade you teach), that's 75 pages a night for you to grade and put in your grade book.

Veteran teachers have figured out plenty of ways to save time. The important thing is this: make sure your methods don't detract from the overall quality of the work your students are turning in.

Option #1: Grade assignments at random. Students still have to do all the work because they never know when you are going to grade something.

Option #2: Have students grade each other's work.

Option #3: Have students present their answers to the class. This will ensure that students are prepared.

There is one other decision you have to make about homework: Why are you giving it? There are several possible reasons:

For Application or Review: Once you teach a concept, you want to give students the opportunity to apply their learning and see if they can do it on their own. To help strengthen students' understanding of a concept they have already learned, they can practice again at home for review.

To Save Time: Students often have work they have to do, like completing the final draft of a writing assignment or reading the next chapter in a book that requires little or no supervision. These activities are often assigned for homework.

Personal Investigation: Every student has his or her own academic interests. These assignments sometimes allow students to explore specific interests within the framework of a certain subject.

For Research: Research that cannot be done in class is often completed somewhere else.

Your students' homework performance will improve if they understand why they are doing it. Explain your reasoning to them. Homework should be purposeful and meaningful.

Things to Consider

Will you give homework every night? How will students (and parents) know what they are expected to do at home?

_____

_____

_____

How much homework will you give?

Schools often have guidelines about the amount of homework they like teachers to assign each night. If your school doesn't, check with other teachers.

_____

_____

_____

Will you have a handout to help students keep track of their homework? What will it look like?

Students may not already have a place for keeping track of their homework. A handout or student planner is an effective way of getting all students to write down their homework for the week; separating the days by subject is also helpful.

_____

_____

_____

How can students make up homework?

_____

_____

_____

Will you grade for completion or for accuracy?

There is no question that students learn more when you grade for accuracy. Try different systems until you find one that holds your students accountable but doesn't keep you up all night.

_____

_____

_____

Will you differentiate homework assignments to meet the needs of all your students?

It is necessary to consider how you will modify assignments for English language learners, below-level students, and above-level students. This helps facilitate achievement for all students.

_____

_____

_____

Will you collect and hand back all homework?

_____

_____

_____

How will you collect homework?

_____

_____

_____

Assessment

Tests and Quizzes

Assessment is a necessary part of instruction and should be conducted regularly. Assessment is the collection of data to measure achievement. It is needed to plan instruction (called formative assessments), to monitor progress along the way, and to assess how well students learned what you taught (called summative assessments). There are many types of testing tools available, including state standardized tests, district-mandated tests, diagnostic tests for your core or basal programs, and informal assessments.

In using the testing process effectively, you will be able to plan your instruction more effectively, targeting what students most need to learn. By assessing what students have learned after you teach, you will also be able to judge how well you taught the material; this will help you improve your teaching methods.

Students perform better on tests when:

- they understand why they are taking the test
- they know the format of the test
- they know several days beforehand when the test will be given
- they know how the test factors into their grades
- they know a variety of test-taking strategies
- they know what will be assessed

Things to Consider

How often will you have tests/quizzes?

_____

Will specific tests always fall on the same day?

Some teachers always have spelling tests on Friday, for example, so that students can get familiar with a schedule. Other teachers like to build flexibility into their testing schedule because they may need extra time for review or to complete a unit of study.

_____

How long will it take you to grade and return tests?

If you take too long to return tests, your students won't get the feedback they need.

_____

Under what circumstances, if any, can your students grade their own tests?

Having students grade their own tests is a great way to save time because they can finish in five minutes what would likely take you hours. One method that some teachers use is to have students answer the questions in pencil and correct them in pen. In addition, students benefit from getting their scores back immediately.

_____

_____

Will you offer makeup tests? Will you factor in time to reteach and retest (for students who need further instruction)?

If the majority of the class does not do well on the test, you may want to reflect on how you taught that particular unit of study. You may need to allow time for reteaching, to teach the content in a different way so that students will understand it.

_____

_____

_____

What are the rules while a test is in progress? What happens if a student breaks one of the rules? Are there circumstances in which you will take points off his or her test? If you suspect someone of cheating, how will you handle it? If the cheating is confirmed, will you give him or her a zero, or have him or her retake the test?

_____

_____

_____

_____

How do you plan to occupy students who finish early?

Students who finish early can sometimes be distracting to the rest of the class. It is best to have something that students can do if they finish early.

_____

_____

_____

How will you inform parents of test grades?

_____

_____

_____

How will you use your assessments to plan instruction?

_____

_____

_____

What types of assessments will you use to monitor progress during a unit of study? How will you know that students are understanding what you are trying to teach them?

_____

_____

_____

What will you do for students who are not receiving passing scores on your tests? What types of interventions can you provide?

_____

_____

_____

Grading

Try to instill in students the understanding that everything they do affects their grades. This includes coming to class on time, paying attention, turning in homework on time and complete, being responsible and respectful, and trying their hardest. A good goal is to motivate students to intrinsically want to do well in school. One way to help do this is to remind students that the decisions they make will affect their grades. You also want them to know that it is never too late to improve their grades.

Your school will ask you to turn in grades for progress reports and report cards at certain times. Most schools give out report cards three or four times a year. It is extremely important that this not be the first time that students and their parents see their grades. Students and their parents must regularly be made aware of how they are doing.

There are two reasons why giving out periodic progress reports is important. First, they serve as motivators for students. Second, they help keep the lines of communication open, thereby avoiding misunderstandings about student progress. When a student is not doing well, some parents react by blaming the teacher. You will want to have proof that you made them aware of their child's grades.

Think carefully before filling in the grade breakdown that follows. A good part of your decision depends on the grade levels and subject(s) you are teaching. For example, in science, a large percentage of one's grade may come from labs and projects. In a subject like drama or music, there may be almost no homework. Primary-grade students will have more emphasis on work done in class, while older students are typically held more accountable for independent work.

How to make sure your students are conscious of their grades:

- Grade and hand back papers promptly.
- Give out periodic progress reports.
- Call parents and inform them of their child's progress.

My Grade Breakdown:

Homework .... _____ %

Tests .... _____ %

Quizzes .... _____ %

Class Participation .... _____ %

Attendance .... _____ %

Projects .... _____ %

Other .... _____ %

Things to Consider

Will you go strictly by the numbers, or will you curve your grades in some way? What is your reasoning?

_____

_____

How will you keep track of class participation and attendance?

_____

_____

When and how will you record your grades?

Most teachers use some kind of grade book, but they are often not designed to record anything more than grades alone. It is helpful to have a book that allows you to see results and progress. Consider including things like attendance, homework, classwork, tests/quizzes, projects, extra credit, and participation. Decide what you want to include for each student. Also think about when you want to record grades; you may decide that certain assignments are great for practice or review but do not need to be recorded. Lastly, decide if you want to use letter grades or numerical scores to show results.

_____

_____

_____

How will you make sure your students know how important their grades are?

_____

_____

_____

How often will you give out progress reports?

Remember that periodic progress reports are a great way to motivate students and keep parents informed. The items you might include on the progress report are the range of time covered by the report, areas of growth, areas to work on, and suggestions for improvement. This also provides a good opportunity to set up a conference time.

_____

_____

How will you recognize students who have done a particularly good job?

Some teachers post a list of high-achieving students, while others do not, out of respect for those not on the list. Others hand out certificates, write letters home, or call home to inform parents. See the Rewards section (pages 49–51) for additional ideas on how to reward students.

_____

_____

_____

How will you warn at-risk students and their parents?

When you call parents to inform them that their child is having challenges at school, make sure you have at least a few positive things to say. Also, be sure to offer some solutions for getting their child back on track.

_____

_____

_____

How can struggling students develop successful strategies?

Developing some kind of work contract may be helpful for student success. This holds the student accountable for assignments by giving a specific due date and a reward for completing the assignment.

_____

_____

_____

Organization

When it comes to teaching, being organized is essential. Being organized means it will take you less time to find the things you need. In other words, organization saves time—and extra time is the one thing that teachers have little of.

Getting organized is much easier if you have a plan. The suggestions below should provide you with the necessary structure.

Tips to Improve Organization:

- Always make extra copies of handouts in case students lose theirs.
- Clip homework and tests together the moment you get them.
- Put papers in the correct place the moment you receive them.
- Hand papers back promptly.

A teacher has to:

- be able to produce certain papers at a moment's notice
- store materials for parents when they come in
- have a record of monthly, weekly, and daily grades
- have materials for those students who are ahead, on task, and behind
- have extra copies in case someone loses his or hers
- store important documents so they can be used next year
- document student behavior in the event that it is needed
- report and submit documents to administration

Things to Consider

Do you have trouble throwing things away? What will you do with the things you want to save?

You may find that clearly marked storage bins and a filing system are the best ways of handling this problem.

_____

_____

_____

Where will you store student work?

Baskets or bins marked "in" and "out" can help organize student work that gets handed in and work that needs to be passed back.

_____

_____

_____

What will you do with student work that has no name on it?

It may be helpful to have a clipboard or basket for these papers, or post them on the board. If a paper does not get claimed by the end of the day, then you might toss it or store it somewhere.

_____

_____

_____

Where will you store your supplies?

If student work and supplies do not need to be easily accessible, you may want to find some way to lock them up.

_____

_____

_____

What materials can you leave at home, and what should be stored at school?

The last thing you want is to arrive at school and realize that you left something important at home, or vice versa. Figure out what you need and where. If you need something in both places, see if you can make a copy, or keep one at school and one at home. Clearly marked storage bins can help distinguish between items/materials for school and items that go home.

_____

_____

_____

How will you keep track of your grades?

Some teachers like grade books because they can carry them around and work on them on the train or at the bus stop. Other teachers put their grades into computer spreadsheets like Excel, which can average your grades at the push of a button. Some districts and schools have required electronic grading systems.

_____

_____

_____

How will you keep track of what you are teaching each day?

A good strategy is to carry a clipboard that has your schedule, lesson plans, and any other important information you might need.

_____

_____

_____

If you are in the middle of a lesson and someone hands you an important paper that you will need later on, what will you do with it?

_____

_____

_____

How will you make sure that anything you might need will be available to you at a moment's notice?

_____

_____

_____

How will you use your home computer to make you more efficient?

Even a simple word-processing program can make life easier. You can copy and paste different sections of lesson plans rather than writing them over. Spreadsheet programs can calculate grades in seconds. Email can make communication with parents easier.

In addition, the Internet is loaded with lesson plans, worksheets, and other resources.

_____

_____

_____

How will you avoid a paper buildup?

Paper buildup exists as one giant pile that contains everything of importance and must be constantly sifted through. Or it consists of many smaller piles that are unorganized and hard to find. Whether you use hanging file folders, paper clips, three-ring binders, file cabinets, or documents scanned into a computer, you should have a system to stay organized.

_____

_____

_____

How will you store things for next year but prevent them from getting in your way?

_____

_____

Supplies

It goes without saying that all students need supplies. However, obtaining supplies is a different challenge for each school. Some schools provide teachers with everything they could possibly need; others provide them with nothing. Some students come from families that can afford to send them to school with an overstuffed backpack, and some come from families that cannot.

Often, parents are willing to donate school supplies to class. You may want to post a "wish list" of items that you would appreciate being donated to your classroom.

Supplies that your students may need:

pencils	tissues	ruler
paper	scissors	erasers
pens	glue	lunchbox
notebooks	smock	folders
crayons	markers	binders
highlighter	calculator	bookbag

What supplies should your students bring with them?

_____

_____

_____

What supplies will you provide?

_____

_____

_____

What will you do if students forget or lose their supplies?

If students forget to bring in their supplies, you don't want them to be unable to work for the whole day. On the other hand, you cannot and should not just give students what they need every time they show up empty-handed. You will need to come up with a consequence for forgetting supplies.

_____

_____

_____

How will you make sure students don't damage their property or the property of others?

Review the Consequences section (pages 45–46) for ideas on enforcing your rules about supplies.

_____

_____

_____

"A place for everything and everything in its place."

— Isabella Beeton

The First Days

If you have gotten this far and you have responded to most or all of the questions, congratulations! Later in the school year, you will look back and be glad you took this time to start thinking about some of the decisions you will be faced with as a new teacher.

However, all this work won't be meaningful unless you share your ideas with your students. It is now time for you to figure out what you are going to do for those first few days. How are you going to make sure you convey everything in this workbook to your students?

Three reasons why the first days of school are for teaching routines and procedures to students:

1. If you ever have a chance to teach your students routines and procedures, this is it!

2. It is easier to establish order early than to restore order later.

3. Your students will learn the habits that you establish early on.

The first days of school are not for teaching subjects. There will be plenty of time later on for academics! When students walk in the door on the first day, greet each one personally. That is just enough time to tell them three things, e.g., your name, how to figure out where they sit, and what they should be doing.

> **The first days are for teaching:**
>
> procedures
>
> routines
>
> rules
>
> consequences
>
> These days are also for creating a sense of community in your classroom and convincing your students that the only way to do well in your class is to work hard.
>
> By focusing on these things, you will be establishing a smooth classroom routine so that the rest of the year can be spent teaching rather than disciplining.

Things to Consider

How and where will you post important information about your class?

Students often feel nervous about finding the correct classroom during the first days of school. Consider posting a sign on the outside of your door with your name, room number, section or period (if appropriate), grade level or subject, and some kind of greeting.

_____

_____

_____

How will you greet your students on the first day?

_____

_____

_____

What activity do you want your students to be doing when they first enter the classroom?

This is an excellent time to give students an activity to do at their seats to keep them occupied while everyone else gets settled. Keep in mind that it may take several minutes for all students to find their classrooms and their seats.

_____

_____

_____

How will you indicate to students where they should sit?

_____

_____

_____

What will be your first words to the class as a whole?

See the following page for an example of what you might say on the first day of school. Remember: What you say on the first day of class will set the tone for the rest of the school year. You don't need to worry about writing out every last word. However, it makes sense to write out the first thing you will say (it may help to write some notes of what you would like to share with the class). If you ever have a time when all your students are listening to you, this is it. Make the most of it.

Example of a Morning Greeting:

Good morning! My name is Mr. Haldeman. Welcome to Class 344! This is my first year in this school.

If you look up on the board, you will see our class motto, "We Are Family." Families work together because they need each other. Look around you; you're going to need these people to succeed. They are your family members.

I hope you'll learn a lot from me this year, but I also hope to learn a lot from you. With that in mind, I'm going to pass around a page to fill out that will give me a better idea of who you are. I'm looking forward to reading them. After all, we're family!

How long do you plan to spend teaching your students rules and procedures?

Some teachers spend many weeks on routines and procedures. Of course, they come up with creative ways to keep it interesting. Some teachers spend one or two weeks. Others simply keep teaching it until they are sure their students have got it. In addition to teaching rules and procedures orally, it is a good idea to post a discipline plan or behavior-management plan somewhere in the classroom where it can be easily seen. Include classroom rules/procedures, consequences, and rewards. You might also create a copy for students that will serve as a contract, to be signed by the student, teacher, and parents.

_____

_____

In what ways will you present the routines and procedures to make them interesting?

_____

_____

_____

How will you check to make sure your students remember the rules and routines?

It is often a good idea to run your students through a refresher course whenever they have come back from a long holiday.

_____

_____

_____

Now it is time to begin planning for the first days of school. Because those first days are so important, you should plan them out as carefully and specifically as possible. On the following page, you will see a sample schedule for the first day of school. Your beginning plans should be just as detailed. Later on, when you feel more comfortable in the classroom, you don't have to be as specific. You can use the blank template on pp. 97–98 to plan for your first day.

> *"What you do on the first days of school will determine your success or failure for the rest of the school year. You will either win or lose your class on the first days of school."*
> —**Harry and Rosemary Wong**

Sample Schedule

Note: This schedule is merely an example and will need to be modified depending on your school and grade level.

Morning

8:15–8:30 Introduction—welcome students, help them find their seats, take roll, and give a brief introduction to the grade level (modeling active listening)

8:30–8:35 Getting to know your teacher (share a little bit about myself)

8:35–9:00 Explain morning routine/procedures (where to line up, how to enter, pledge of allegiance, where to turn in papers, what to get started on, attendance, etc.)

9:00–9:15 Why this school is special (a class discussion), followed by an explanation of our class motto: "We Are Family"

9:15–9:45 "Getting to Know You" activity (followed by sharing) or, for younger students, a tour of the school to show important locations

9:45–9:50 Procedure for collecting papers (passer, collector, use paper clips)

9:50–10:00 Distribute supplies

10:00–10:15 Explanation of behavior expectations

10:15–10:25 Rules and signals (explain the stoplight)

10:25–10:30 Restroom and Tardy Policies

10:30–10:45 Recess/Snack break

10:45–11:00 Exercise on Rule #1 (Listen and Speak with Respect)

11:00–11:30 Brainstorm about classroom consequences and rewards (make list on board)

11:30–11:40 Lunch procedure (how to exit) and walking-in-line procedure

11:40–12:25 Lunch

Afternoon

12:25–1:00 Return-from-lunch procedure (something on desk or board to do); Goals for the year (rough draft—3 to 5 sentences)

1:00–1:45 Classroom community activity (Create a puzzle of the classroom number out of poster board; have each student decorate a piece of the puzzle and reassemble the puzzle. For older students, create a word or number puzzle for students to solve as a class.)

1:45–1:55 Discuss the importance of working together throughout the year

1:55–2:15 Grading system and homework policy

2:15–2:20 Parent/student/teacher contract

2:20–2:30 Dismissal procedure

2:30–2:40 End of the day recap

2:40–2:45 Lineup and dismissal

My Schedule: Day 1

Morning

Time   **Activity**

__ – __   _____

__ – __   _____

__ – __   _____

__ – __   _____

__ – __   _____

__ – __   _____

__ – __   _____

__ – __   _____

__ – __   _____

__ – __   _____

__ – __   _____

__ – __   _____

__ – __   _____

__ – __   _____

__ – __   _____

__ – __   _____

__ – __   _____

__ – __   _____

__ – __   _____

Afternoon

Time	Activity
___ – ___	_____
___ – ___	_____
___ – ___	_____
___ – ___	_____
___ – ___	_____
___ – ___	_____
___ – ___	_____
___ – ___	_____
___ – ___	_____
___ – ___	_____
___ – ___	_____
___ – ___	_____

More to Consider

The following is a list of additional items you may have questions about for your school principal or for other staff members as you get started with your first year:

- How to schedule a Student Study Team (SST)

- Procedures for lunch, lunch line, money for buying lunch or computer codes if money is no longer used

- School bell schedule

- Procedures for referring a child to the office/principal

- Schoolwide systems like school money or "blue slips" used on the playground to advise teachers of an incident

- Procedures for sending a child to the nurse

- How to use the phone or contact the office

- Procedure for obtaining/ordering new supplies

- Booking field trips (which often has to be done at the beginning of the year), district or school policy on collecting money for field trips, school money available for field trips

- District/school policy for asking for supplies or donations

- What support is available for new teachers

- Do I have all the curriculum that I am supposed to have? Where can I obtain it if something is missing?

- Do I have enough books for my students? Where can I obtain more? Is there a checkout procedure that the teacher needs to be aware of?

- Yard-duty, bus-stop duty, and gate-duty schedules

- Adjunct duty

- Are there benchmark tests or other district assessments that I will be responsible for administering? Are there cutoff dates for when to give them by?

- Where are the cumulative files (often called "cums")? How can I access them to learn about my students? What is my responsibility for updating them? Do I need to do that at the beginning, middle, or end of the year?

- Is there a master school calendar with dates I should be aware of, such as assembly dates, progress reports/report cards sent home, and conferences?

- Are there other responsibilities that I have at the school that I should know about?

Conclusion

Congratulations! You have taken a great first step toward being prepared for the upcoming school year. You have just made dozens of decisions about how you want your room to look, what kind of teacher you want to be, what rules and procedures you will have, and many other important things. Here are some parting words: Keep this book handy!

As the year progresses, you may change some of the things in this book or rewrite/erase other things. That is perfectly natural. In fact, it is necessary. Things may change in the classroom, and over time, you will have a better idea of what works and what doesn't.

You have just completed a significant portion of the planning that a first-year teacher does. Use this book as a reference guide to help you remember some of your initial ideas. If you worry, for instance, that you are not being consistent with your consequences, go back and remind yourself of what you wrote in that section.

Teaching is a skill. It is not something you are born with. Like anything in life, the better prepared you are, the more successful you will be.

Your first year as a new teacher will be an intense experience. It will be trying, eye-opening, busy, and wonderful. Focus on the positives as much as you can. Every day that you wake up and go to school, you will be a better teacher than you were the day before.

It will be an amazing journey.

"Education is not preparation for life; education is life itself."

—John Dewey

References Cited

Beeton, I. 1861. *Mrs. Beeton's household management.* London: S. O. Beeton. http://www.mrsbeeton.com

Darling-Hammond, L., and J. Baratz-Snowden, eds. 2007. A good teacher in every classroom: Preparing the highly qualified teachers our children deserve. *Educational Horizons* 85 (2): 111–132.

Dewey, J. 1992. In *Familiar quotations.* 16th ed. Ed. J. Bartlett and J. Kaplan. London: Little, Brown.

Jones, F. 2000. *Tools for teaching.* Santa Cruz, CA: Fredric H. Jones & Associates, Inc.

Quinn, D. Quotations on teaching, learning, and education. Website compiled by the National Teaching and Learning Forum and published by James Rhem & Associates, LLC. http:// www.ntlf.com/html/lib/quotes.htm.

Rouk, U. 1980. What makes an effective teacher? *American Educator: The Professional Journal of the American Federation of Teachers* 4 (3): 14–17, 33.

Saphier, J., and R. Gower. 1997. *The skillful teacher, building your teaching skills.* 5th ed. Carlisle, MA: Research for Better Teaching, Inc.

Wong, H. K., and R. T. Wong. 2004. *The first days of school: How to be an effective teacher.* Mountain View, CA: Harry K. Wong Publications, Inc.

U.S. Department of Education. 2006. *The secretary's fifth annual report on teacher quality: A highly qualified teacher in every classroom.* Washington, D.C.

Notes

Notes